D1146032

FOR THE
BEST MUM
IN THE
WORLD

summersdale

FOR THE BEST MUM IN THE WORLD

Summersdale Publishers Ltd
46 West Street
Chichester
West Sussex
PO19 1RP
UK

www.summersdale.com

Printed and bound in the Czech Republic

ISBN: 978-1-84953-526-7

Substantial discounts on bulk quantities of Summersdale books are available to corporations, professional associations and other organisations. For details telephone Nicky Douglas on (+44-1243-756902), fax (+44-1243-786300) or email (nicky@summersdale.com).

TO...

FROM.......................................

ALL THAT I AM, OR EVER
HOPE TO BE, I OWE TO MY
ANGEL MOTHER.

Abraham Lincoln

A MOTHER'S HAPPINESS
IS LIKE A BEACON,
LIGHTING UP THE
FUTURE BUT REFLECTED
ALSO ON THE PAST IN
THE GUISE OF FOND
MEMORIES.

Honoré de Balzac

THERE IS A POINT AT
WHICH YOU AREN'T
AS MUCH MOM AND
DAUGHTER AS YOU ARE
ADULTS AND FRIENDS.

Jamie Lee Curtis

SHE WAS THE BEST
OF ALL MOTHERS, TO
WHOM, FOR BODY AND
SOUL I OWE ENDLESS
GRATITUDE.

Thomas Carlyle

CHILDREN AND MOTHERS
NEVER TRULY PART —
BOUND IN THE BEATING
OF EACH OTHER'S HEART.

Charlotte Gray

MOTHER IS THE
HEARTBEAT IN THE
HOME; AND WITHOUT
HER, THERE SEEMS TO
BE NO HEART THROB.

Leroy Brownlow

MY LIFE BEGAN WITH
WAKING UP AND LOVING
MY MOTHER'S FACE.

George Eliot

TO A CHILD'S EAR,
'MOTHER' IS MAGIC IN
ANY LANGUAGE.

Arlene Benedict

THERE WAS NEVER A
GREAT MAN WHO HAD
NOT A GREAT MOTHER
— IT IS HARDLY AN
EXAGGERATION.

Olive Schreiner

YOUTH FADES, LOVE
DROOPS, THE LEAVES OF
FRIENDSHIP FALL;
A MOTHER'S SECRET
HOPE OUTLIVES
THEM ALL.

Oliver Wendell Holmes Sr

YOU MAKE
EVERYTHING
BETTER

HEAVEN IS AT THE FEET OF MOTHERS.

Arabic proverb

ONLY MOTHERS
CAN THINK OF THE
FUTURE — BECAUSE
THEY GIVE BIRTH TO IT
IN THEIR CHILDREN.

Maxim Gorky

A MOTHER'S ARMS ARE MORE COMFORTING THAN ANYONE ELSE'S.

Diana, Princess of Wales

ANYONE WHO DOESN'T MISS THE PAST NEVER HAD A MOTHER.

Gregory Nunn

IT SEEMS TO ME
MY MOTHER WAS THE
MOST SPLENDID WOMAN
I EVER KNEW.

Charlie Chaplin

A MOTHER IS NOT A PERSON TO LEAN ON, BUT A PERSON TO MAKE LEANING UNNECESSARY.

Dorothy Canfield Fisher

MOTHERHOOD IN ALL ITS GUISES AND PERMUTATIONS IS MORE ART THAN SCIENCE.

Melinda M. Marshall

FOR WHEN A CHILD IS
BORN THE MOTHER ALSO
IS BORN AGAIN.

Gilbert Parker

GOD COULD NOT BE EVERYWHERE, SO HE CREATED MOTHERS.

Jewish proverb

ALL MOTHERLY LOVE IS REALLY WITHOUT REASON AND LOGIC.

Joan Chen

THE MOST BEAUTIFUL
WORD ON THE LIPS OF
MANKIND IS THE WORD
'MOTHER'.

Kahlil Gibran

BEAUTIFUL AS WAS
MAMMA'S FACE, IT
BECAME INCOMPARABLY
MORE LOVELY WHEN SHE
SMILED, AND SEEMED TO
ENLIVEN EVERYTHING
ABOUT HER.

Leo Tolstoy

YOU GIVE THE
BEST HUGS

ALL MOTHERS ARE RICH
WHEN THEY LOVE THEIR
CHILDREN... THERE ARE
NO POOR MOTHERS, NO
UGLY ONES, NO
OLD ONES.

Maurice Maeterlinck

SWEATER, N.:
GARMENT WORN BY
CHILD WHEN ITS MOTHER
IS FEELING CHILLY.

Ambrose Bierce

GOVERN A FAMILY
AS YOU WOULD COOK
A SMALL FISH —
VERY GENTLY.

Chinese proverb

THERE IS NO VELVET
SO SOFT AS A MOTHER'S
LAP, NO ROSE AS LOVELY
AS HER SMILE, NO PATH
SO FLOWERY AS THAT
IMPRINTED WITH HER
FOOTSTEPS.

Edward Thomson

MOTHER'S LOVE IS BLISS,
IS PEACE, IT NEED NOT
BE ACQUIRED, IT NEED
NOT BE DESERVED.

Erich Fromm

OUR MOTHERS ALWAYS
REMAIN THE STRANGEST,
CRAZIEST PEOPLE WE'VE
EVER MET.

Marguerite Duras

A MOTHER HOLDS
HER CHILDREN'S HANDS
FOR A WHILE, THEIR
HEARTS FOREVER.

Anonymous

ANY MOTHER
COULD PERFORM THE
JOBS OF SEVERAL AIR
TRAFFIC CONTROLLERS
WITH EASE.

Lisa Alther

ALWAYS BE NICE TO YOUR
CHILDREN BECAUSE
THEY ARE THE ONES
WHO WILL CHOOSE YOUR
REST HOME.

Phyllis Diller

AN OUNCE OF MOTHER IS WORTH A POUND OF CLERGY.

Proverb

THERE IS NO WAY TO BE
A PERFECT MOTHER,
AND A MILLION WAYS TO
BE A GOOD ONE.

Jill Churchill

MOTHER IS THE ONE
WE COUNT ON FOR THE
THINGS THAT MATTER
MOST OF ALL.

Katharine Butler Hathaway

MAKING THE DECISION
TO HAVE A CHILD IS
MOMENTOUS. IT IS TO
DECIDE FOREVER TO
HAVE YOUR HEART
GO WALKING AROUND
OUTSIDE YOUR BODY.

Elizabeth Stone

NO PAINTER'S
BRUSH, NOR POET'S
PEN IN JUSTICE TO
HER FAME HAS EVER
REACHED HALF HIGH
ENOUGH TO WRITE A
MOTHER'S NAME.

Anonymous

YOU'RE ALWAYS
THERE FOR ME

A WOMAN IS LIKE A
TEABAG. YOU CAN'T TELL
HOW STRONG SHE IS
UNTIL YOU PUT HER IN
HOT WATER.

Anonymous

THERE ARE TWO THINGS
WE SHOULD GIVE OUR
CHILDREN. ONE IS ROOTS
AND THE OTHER
IS WINGS.

Hodding Carter

MOTHER IS THE
NAME FOR GOD IN THE
LIPS AND HEARTS OF
LITTLE CHILDREN.

William Makepeace Thackeray

TO DESCRIBE MY MOTHER
WOULD BE TO WRITE
ABOUT A HURRICANE IN
ITS PERFECT POWER.

Maya Angelou

THE PATIENCE OF A
MOTHER MIGHT BE
LIKENED TO A TUBE
OF TOOTHPASTE — IT'S
NEVER QUITE ALL GONE.

Anonymous

THERE IS ONLY ONE
PRETTY CHILD IN THE
WORLD, AND EVERY
MOTHER HAS IT.

Chinese proverb

BIOLOGY IS THE LEAST OF WHAT MAKES SOMEONE A MOTHER.

Oprah Winfrey

FOR THE HAND THAT
ROCKS THE CRADLE
IS THE HAND THAT
RULES THE WORLD.

William Ross Wallace

I CANNOT TELL HOW
MUCH I OWE TO THE
SOLEMN WORDS OF MY
GOOD MOTHER.

Charles Spurgeon

WOMANLINESS MEANS
ONLY MOTHERHOOD;
ALL LOVE BEGINS AND
ENDS THERE.

Robert Browning

A MOTHER ALWAYS HAS
TO THINK TWICE, ONCE
FOR HERSELF AND ONCE
FOR HER CHILD.

Sophia Loren

AT THAT BEST ACADEME,
A MOTHER'S KNEE.

James Russell Lowell

YOU MAKE ME FEEL SPECIAL AND LOVED

ALL WOMEN BECOME LIKE
THEIR MOTHERS. THAT IS
THEIR TRAGEDY. NO MAN
DOES. THAT'S HIS.

Oscar Wilde

MOST OF ALL THE OTHER
BEAUTIFUL THINGS IN
LIFE COME BY TWOS AND
THREES, BY DOZENS AND
HUNDREDS. PLENTY OF
ROSES, STARS, SUNSETS,
RAINBOWS... BUT ONLY
ONE MOTHER IN THE
WHOLE WORLD.

Kate Douglas Wiggin

SOMETIMES THE
STRENGTH OF
MOTHERHOOD IS
GREATER THAN
NATURAL LAWS.

Barbara Kingsolver

A MAN LOVES HIS
SWEETHEART THE MOST,
HIS WIFE THE BEST,
BUT HIS MOTHER
THE LONGEST.

Irish proverb

WHEN A CHILD NEEDS A MOTHER TO TALK TO, NOBODY ELSE BUT A MOTHER WILL DO.

Erica Jong

THE NATURAL STATE
OF MOTHERHOOD IS
UNSELFISHNESS.

Jessica Lange

A MOTHER IS A MOTHER
STILL,
THE HOLIEST THING
ALIVE.

Samuel Taylor Coleridge

ALL THAT I AM MY MOTHER MADE ME.

John Quincy Adams

MY MOTHER'S LOVE FOR
ME WAS SO GREAT I
HAVE WORKED HARD TO
JUSTIFY IT.

Marc Chagall

SHE NEVER QUITE
LEAVES HER CHILDREN
AT HOME, EVEN WHEN
SHE DOESN'T TAKE
THEM ALONG.

Margaret Culkin Banning

THE GOD TO WHOM
LITTLE BOYS SAY THEIR
PRAYERS HAS A FACE
VERY LIKE THEIR
MOTHER'S.

J. M. Barrie

WHAT DO GIRLS DO WHO HAVEN'T ANY MOTHERS TO HELP THEM THROUGH THEIR TROUBLES?

Louisa May Alcott

A MOM'S HUG LASTS LONG AFTER SHE LETS GO.

Anonymous

MY MOTHER IS A
WALKING MIRACLE.

Leonardo DiCaprio

YOU ALWAYS SEE THE BEST IN EVERYTHING I DO

A MOTHER'S ARMS ARE
MADE OF TENDERNESS
AND CHILDREN SLEEP
SOUNDLY IN THEM.

Victor Hugo

WHERE THERE IS A
MOTHER IN THE HOME,
MATTERS GO WELL.

Amos Bronson Alcott

A MOTHER IS SHE WHO CAN TAKE THE PLACE OF ALL OTHERS BUT WHOSE PLACE NO ONE ELSE CAN TAKE.

Gaspard Mermillod

AS A PARENT YOU TRY
TO MAINTAIN A CERTAIN
AMOUNT OF CONTROL
AND SO YOU HAVE THIS
TUG OF WAR... YOU HAVE
TO LEARN WHEN
TO LET GO.

Aretha Franklin

THE BEST WAY TO KEEP
CHILDREN AT HOME IS
TO MAKE THE HOME
ATMOSPHERE PLEASANT,
AND LET THE AIR OUT OF
THE TYRES.

Dorothy Parker

A MOTHER UNDERSTANDS WHAT A CHILD DOES NOT SAY.

Jewish proverb

THE ONLY MOTHERS IT
IS SAFE TO FORGET ON
MOTHER'S DAY ARE THE
GOOD ONES.

Mignon McLaughlin

SHE'S BEAUTIFUL AESTHETICALLY, BUT SHE IS A BEAUTIFUL MOTHER TOO.

Kate Hudson
on her mother

A MOTHER... SEEING
THERE ARE ONLY FOUR
PIECES OF PIE FOR
FIVE PEOPLE, PROMPTLY
ANNOUNCES SHE NEVER
DID CARE FOR PIE.

Tenneva Jordan

THINK OF YOUR MOTHER AND SMILE FOR ALL OF THE GOOD PRECIOUS MOMENTS.

Ana Monnar

A SMART MOTHER
MAKES OFTEN A BETTER
DIAGNOSIS THAN A
POOR DOCTOR.

August Bier

THE PHRASE 'WORKING MOTHER' IS REDUNDANT.

Jane Sellman

YOU'RE ALWAYS
LOOKING OUT
FOR ME

MEN ARE WHAT THEIR MOTHERS MADE THEM.

Ralph Waldo Emerson

MOTHERS... WHO CARRY
THE KEY OF OUR SOULS
IN THEIR BOSOMS.

Oliver Wendell Holmes Sr

MY MOTHER MADE
A BRILLIANT IMPRESSION
UPON MY CHILDHOOD
LIFE. SHE SHONE
FOR ME LIKE THE
EVENING STAR.

Winston Churchill

WHEN YOU LOOK
AT YOUR MOTHER, YOU
ARE LOOKING AT THE
PUREST LOVE YOU WILL
EVER KNOW.

Mitch Albom

IF LOVE IS SWEET AS
A FLOWER, THEN MY
MOTHER IS THAT SWEET
FLOWER OF LOVE.

Stevie Wonder

THE ART OF MOTHERING IS TO TEACH THE ART OF LIVING TO CHILDREN.

Elaine Heffner

MOST MOTHERS
ARE INSTINCTIVE
PHILOSOPHERS.

Harriet Beecher Stowe

THAT WAS THE BANK WHERE WE DEPOSITED ALL OUR HURTS AND WORRIES.

Thomas De Witt Talmage
on his mother

A MOTHER'S LOVE
PERCEIVES NO
IMPOSSIBILITIES.

Cornelia Paddock

A MOTHER IS ONE TO WHOM YOU HURRY WHEN YOU ARE TROUBLED.

Emily Dickinson

MY MOTHER'S WONDERFUL. TO ME SHE'S PERFECTION.

Michael Jackson

I KNOW ENOUGH TO
KNOW THAT WHEN
YOU'RE IN A PICKLE...
CALL MOM.

Jennifer Garner

YOU LISTEN TO
ALL MY STORIES

SOME MOTHERS ARE
KISSING MOTHERS AND
SOME ARE SCOLDING
MOTHERS... MOST
MOTHERS KISS AND
SCOLD TOGETHER.

Pearl S. Buck

WHO RAN TO HELP
ME WHEN I FELL,
AND WOULD SOME
PRETTY STORY TELL,
OR KISS THE PLACE TO
MAKE IT WELL?
MY MOTHER.

Ann Taylor

SOMETIMES THE
LAUGHTER IN MOTHERING
IS THE RECOGNITION
OF THE IRONIES AND
ABSURDITIES. SOMETIMES,
THOUGH, IT'S JUST PURE,
UNTHINKING DELIGHT.

Barbara Schapiro

A MOTHER'S HEART IS A
PATCHWORK OF LOVE.

Anonymous

STORIES FIRST HEARD
AT A MOTHER'S KNEE
ARE NEVER WHOLLY
FORGOTTEN.

Giovanni Ruffini

A MOTHER'S HEART IS ALWAYS WITH HER CHILDREN.

Proverb

I SHALL NEVER
FORGET MY MOTHER,
FOR IT WAS SHE WHO
PLANTED AND NURTURED
THE FIRST SEEDS OF
GOOD WITHIN ME.

Immanuel Kant

MOTHER'S LOVE GROWS BY GIVING.

Charles Lamb

A PARENT'S LOVE IS WHOLE NO MATTER HOW MANY TIMES DIVIDED.

Robert Brault

A MOTHER'S LOVE FOR
HER CHILD IS LIKE
NOTHING ELSE IN
THE WORLD.

Agatha Christie

THE TIE WHICH LINKS
MOTHER AND CHILD
IS OF SUCH PURE AND
IMMACULATE STRENGTH
AS TO BE NEVER
VIOLATED.

Washington Irving

ALL MOTHERS ARE
QUINTESSENTIAL: IN
PAIN AND JOY THEY
ARE ALWAYS WITH
US, ENCOURAGING,
INSTRUCTING, LOVING.

Peter Megargee Brown

MOTHERHOOD IS AT ITS
BEST WHEN THE TENDER
CHORDS OF SYMPATHY
HAVE BEEN TOUCHED.

Paul Harris

IF EVOLUTION REALLY WORKS, HOW COME MOTHERS ONLY HAVE TWO HANDS?

Milton Berle

YOU ALWAYS
KNOW HOW TO
CHEER ME UP

IF MEN HAD TO HAVE BABIES, THEY WOULD ONLY EVER HAVE ONE EACH.

Diana, Princess of Wales

THE PASSION OF LOVE IS
ESSENTIALLY SELFISH,
WHILE MOTHERHOOD
WIDENS THE CIRCLE OF
OUR FEELINGS.

Honoré de Balzac

WHEN YOU ARE A MOTHER, YOU ARE NEVER REALLY ALONE IN YOUR THOUGHTS.

Sophia Loren

IF YOU HAVE A MOM,
THERE IS NOWHERE
YOU ARE LIKELY TO GO
WHERE A PRAYER HAS
NOT ALREADY BEEN.

Robert Brault

MY MOTHER HAD A
GREAT DEAL OF TROUBLE
WITH ME, BUT I THINK
SHE ENJOYED IT.

Mark Twain

MOTHER IS FAR TOO
CLEVER TO UNDERSTAND
ANYTHING SHE DOES
NOT LIKE.

Arnold Bennett

THE MOTHER'S HEART IS THE CHILD'S SCHOOLROOM.

Henry Ward Beecher

MY MOTHER'S GREAT...
SHE COULD STOP YOU
FROM DOING ANYTHING,
THROUGH A CLOSED
DOOR EVEN, WITH A
SINGLE LOOK.

Whoopi Goldberg

WHATEVER ELSE IS
UNSURE IN THIS...
WORLD A MOTHER'S
LOVE IS NOT.

James Joyce

SHE MAY SCOLD YOU
FOR LITTLE THINGS,
BUT NEVER FOR THE
BIG ONES.

Harry S. Truman

A MOTHER IS THE TRUEST FRIEND WE HAVE.

Washington Irving

MOTHERS... SPEAK
THE SAME TONGUE. A
MOTHER IN MANCHURIA
COULD CONVERSE WITH
A MOTHER IN NEBRASKA
AND NEVER MISS A WORD.

Will Rogers

YOU'RE MY BEST
FRIEND, AS WELL
AS MY MOTHER

PRIDE IS ONE OF THE
SEVEN DEADLY SINS; BUT
IT CANNOT BE THE PRIDE
OF A MOTHER IN HER
CHILDREN, FOR THAT
IS A COMPOUND OF TWO
CARDINAL VIRTUES –
FAITH AND HOPE.

Charles Dickens

NOTHING BEATS HAVING
THIS BEAUTIFUL CHILD
LOOK AT ME AND SAY,
'MUM'.

Nicole Appleton

FOR THIRTY YEARS
SHE SERVED THE
FAMILY NOTHING
BUT LEFTOVERS. THE
ORIGINAL MEAL HAS
NEVER BEEN FOUND.

Calvin Trillin

THERE IS A POWER THAT COMES TO WOMEN WHEN THEY GIVE BIRTH.

Sheryl Feldman

I THOUGHT MY MUM'S
WHOLE PURPOSE WAS TO
BE MY MOM. THAT'S HOW
SHE MADE ME FEEL.

Natasha Gregson Wagner

YOU WILL ALWAYS BE YOUR CHILD'S FAVOURITE TOY.

Vicki Lansky

THE GREATEST LOVE IS A MOTHER'S; THEN A DOG'S; THEN A SWEETHEART'S.

Polish proverb

WHAT IS A HOME WITHOUT CHILDREN? QUIET.

Henny Youngman

ALL I KNOW IS THAT
WHEN I'M A PARENT I
WANT TO BE JUST LIKE
MY MOM.

Nikki Reed

WHAT IS MOTHERHOOD SAVE NATURE IN HER MOST GLADSOME MOOD?

Honoré de Balzac

THE SWEETEST SOUNDS TO MORTALS GIVEN ARE HEARD IN MOTHER, HOME, AND HEAVEN.

William Goldsmith Brown

THERE NEVER WAS A
CHILD SO LOVELY, BUT
HIS MOTHER WAS GLAD
TO GET HIM ASLEEP.

Ralph Waldo Emerson

THERE IS NO
RECIPROCITY. MEN LOVE
WOMEN, WOMEN LOVE
CHILDREN. CHILDREN
LOVE HAMSTERS.

Alice Thomas Ellis

A LITTLE GIRL, ASKED
WHERE HER HOME
WAS, REPLIED, 'WHERE
MOTHER IS.'

Keith L. Brooks

IMAGINATION IS
SOMETHING THAT SITS
UP WITH DAD AND MOM
THE FIRST TIME THEIR
TEENAGER STAYS
OUT LATE.

Lane Olinghouse

GROWN DON'T MEAN
NOTHING TO A MOTHER.

Toni Morrison

IT KILLS YOU TO SEE
THEM GROW UP. BUT I
GUESS IT WOULD KILL
YOU QUICKER IF
THEY DIDN'T.

Barbara Kingsolver

THERE'S NO ROAD MAP
ON HOW TO RAISE A
FAMILY: IT'S ALWAYS AN
ENORMOUS NEGOTIATION.

Meryl Streep

THE MOST CONSISTENT GIFT AND BURDEN OF MOTHERHOOD IS ADVICE.

Susan Chira

ONE GOOD MOTHER IS
WORTH A HUNDRED
SCHOOLMASTERS.

George Herbert

I KNOW HOW TO DO ANYTHING — I'M A MOM.

Roseanne Barr

BEHIND ALL YOUR
STORIES IS ALWAYS
YOUR MOTHER'S STORY,
BECAUSE HERS IS WHERE
YOURS BEGINS.

Mitch Albom

HUNDREDS OF DEWDROPS
TO GREET THE DAWN;
HUNDREDS OF LAMBS IN
THE PURPLE CLOVER;
HUNDREDS OF
BUTTERFLIES ON
THE LAWN;
BUT ONLY ONE MOTHER
THE WIDE WORLD OVER.

George Cooper

NO INFLUENCE IS SO POWERFUL AS THAT OF THE MOTHER.

James Black

A CHILD EDUCATED
ONLY AT SCHOOL IS AN
UNEDUCATED CHILD.

George Santayana

THE ONLY LOVE
THAT I REALLY BELIEVE
IN IS A MOTHER'S LOVE
FOR HER CHILDREN.

Karl Lagerfeld

THE WATCHFUL
MOTHER TARRIES NIGH,
THOUGH SLEEP
HAVE CLOSED HER
INFANT'S EYE.

John Keble

MOTHERS ALWAYS KNOW.

Oprah Winfrey

I CAN ALWAYS
TURN TO YOU

IN A CHILD'S EYES, A MOTHER IS A GODDESS.

N. K. Jemisin

WHILE WE TRY TO TEACH
OUR CHILDREN ABOUT
LIFE, OUR CHILDREN
TEACH US WHAT LIFE
IS ALL ABOUT.

Angela Schwindt

THOU ART THY MOTHER'S
GLASS, AND SHE IN THEE
CALLS BACK THE LOVELY
APRIL OF HER PRIME.

William Shakespeare

OF ALL THE RIGHTS OF
WOMEN, THE GREATEST
IS TO BE A MOTHER.

Lin Yutang

NO LANGUAGE CAN
EXPRESS THE POWER AND
BEAUTY AND HEROISM OF
A MOTHER'S LOVE.

E. H. Chapin

YOU'RE THE
BEST MUM IN
THE WORLD!

@EsmeTheBird

If you're interested in finding out more about our books, find us on Facebook at **Summersdale Publishers** and follow us on Twitter at **@Summersdale**.

www.summersdale.com